MW01110446

# LANCE
# ARMSTRONG

Gloria D. Miklowitz

⫶ Dominie Press, Inc.

**Publisher:** Raymond Yuen
**Editor:** Bob Rowland
**Designer:** Greg DiGenti
**Photo Credits:** Reuters/Corbis (cover and pages 13, 25, 29, and 33); and Duomo/Corbis (Page 8)

Published by:

🔁 **Dominie Press, Inc.**

1949 Kellogg Avenue
Carlsbad, California 92008 USA

www.dominie.com

Paperback ISBN 0-7685-3044-X
Library Bound Edition ISBN 0-7685-3571-9
Printed in Singapore by PH Productions Pte Ltd
1 2 3 4 5 PH 07 06 05

# Table of Contents

Chapter 1
**"You Have to Believe"**...........................5

Chapter 2
**Racing toward a Bright Future** ........11

Chapter 3
**A Dark Cloud of Cancer**.....................17

Chapter 4
**Ready for the Tour de France** ..........21

Chapter 5
**"A Simple Pleasure"** ...........................26

Glossary ................................................35

# "You Have to Believe"

**W**hat drove Lance Armstrong to become the world's greatest bicyclist? What pushed him to triumph over both cancer and the Tour de France, the most popular sporting event in Europe? And what drove him to win a record-breaking six years in a row?

"Anything is possible," Lance said. "You can be told that you have a 90 percent chance or a 50 percent chance or a 1 percent chance, but you have to believe, and you have to fight."

Lance Armstrong was born in Plano, Texas, on September 18, 1971. His mother, Linda, was only seventeen when he was born. His father left Linda before Lance was two years old. "I never had a real father, but I never sat around wishing for one, either," Lance wrote in his autobiography, *It's not About the Bike*.

For a while they lived in a dreary apartment while Linda worked part time and finished school. At first she made $400 a month. Rent cost $200 and daycare was $25 a week, but Lance said she gave him everything he needed.

When Lance was three, his mother married again. Her husband, Terry Armstrong, had a bad temper and frequently hit Lance with a thick, wooden paddle. Not that Lance was always the model child. He was willful, always testing the boundaries. And he didn't like to take advice. Still, his stepfather legally adopted him and gave him his last name. By the time Lance was in his teens, however, Linda divorced Terry Armstrong.

A highlight of Lance's early years was getting his first bicycle at the age of seven. He loved it. "A bike is freedom to roam without rules and without adults," he wrote in his autobiography.

In Plano, "if you weren't a football player, you didn't exist; and if you weren't upper middle class, you might as well not exist, either," Lance said.

But he wasn't good at football, and he wasn't upper middle class.

In fifth grade, he decided that he wanted very much to succeed at *something*. He entered a distance running race and told his mother, "I'm going to be a champ." She gave him a 1972 silver dollar for good luck and said, "Now, remember, all you have to do is beat that clock." He won the race.

Next, Lance joined the local swim club, even though he didn't know how to swim. He was twelve at the time, but he was placed with the seven-year-old swimmers. He didn't swim with the younger group for long. In a year he was fourth in his age group in the state in the 1,500-meter freestyle. How did he become such a good swimmer? He

◀ *Lance Armstrong races in the first New York City Cycling Championship, which he won, in August 2002*

trained very hard. He'd ride his bike ten miles to be at the swimming pool for a 5:30 A.M. workout before going to school. After school, it was back to the pool for more workouts, and then the bike ride home. That meant six miles in the pool and twenty miles on the bike.

One day, when Lance was about thirteen, he saw a flyer for a triathlon race called Iron Kids. The event combined bike riding, swimming, and running—all things he did well. He signed up for the race, and his mother bought him a triathlon outfit and his first sleek racing bike.

Without special training for the Iron Kids triathlon, he won!

Soon after that, Lance entered and won another triathlon in Houston, Texas. Winning made him feel great. At last he found a way to win.

Chapter 2

# Racing toward a Bright Future

**W**hen Lance was fifteen, he entered the 1987 President's Triathlon against hundreds of experienced, older competitors. He finished thirty-second and told a reporter that within ten years he would be "the best." Some of his friends thought he was being arrogant.

The following year, at age sixteen, he finished fifth.

The races and triathlons paid well, and Lance entered as many as possible. When he was still in high school he was earning about $20,000 a year in prize money. He was even able to buy a car. He began to realize he had a future as an athlete.

Lance's remarkable ability came to the attention of the Cooper Institute, in Dallas, Texas. They invited him to go there to test his lung capacity. His levels were the highest ever recorded at the clinic. And his heart was almost one-third larger than an average man's. At rest it beat only about thirty-two times a minute. When he's exercising hard, his rate can go up above 200 beats a minute!

To keep in shape between races, Lance ran six miles every day and then

*Lance Armstrong leads the pack
in the 2002 Tour de France*

rode his bike into the evening. He had
two sets of friends: popular high school
kids he'd hang around with, and athletic
friends, some of them grown men.

When he was a senior in high
school, Lance entered an important

13

time trial for young riders in New Mexico. It was a twelve-mile flat course. On the morning of the race he was up at six o'clock to warm up. It was very cold outside. Staying warm for a time trial is critical because you have to be ready to peddle hard as soon as the officials shout, "Go!" When he told his mother he forgot to pack a jacket, she offered him her small pink jacket, which barely covered him. Still cold, in the last minutes before the race began, he sat in their car with the heater on full blast, and then jumped onto his bike. He beat the course record by forty-five seconds.

It became clear that Lance might make it as a world-class athlete, but there were obstacles. When he was invited to train with the junior U.S. national team and go to Moscow, Russia, for the 1990

Junior World Championship race, officials at his high school told him he couldn't graduate if he missed six weeks of schoolwork. Not one to be easily discouraged, Lance's mother found a high school that would allow Lance to graduate if he'd take a few make-up classes.

Chris Carmichael, the director of the U.S. national cycling team, wanted to develop a winning squad of American cyclists. He recognized Lance's remarkable ability. Even though he was still a teenager, Lance's body seemed especially designed for cycling. When Chris became Lance's coach, he found him to be too boastful. "Lance relied on his gift," Chris said. He didn't listen when Chris instructed him to break away from the other cyclists close to the end of the race. Instead, he got out in front too early and ran out of steam for the final push to the finish line. What he had yet to learn was that the top riders were as strong, if not stronger, than he was; as a result, tactics and technique were important. That's what Chris would teach him.

By 1991, after several years of improving performances, Lance became the U.S. amateur champion. In 1992 he turned professional. A year later he became the youngest man ever to win both a stage (each day in a race is called a stage) in the Tour de France and the World Road Championship.

He was only twenty-two, and Lance Armstrong's future looked brighter than he had ever dreamed.

# Chapter 3

# A Dark Cloud of Cancer

For months, Lance trained for and competed in European races. Over long hours, his feet were clamped to the pedals of his bike. He often burned 6,000 calories a day and jounced over cobblestones, up and down steep mountains in rain, snow, and terrible heat. At night he roomed with two or three other cyclists in cheap hotels, eating food he didn't like.

"You don't win a race all on your own," Lance wrote in his autobiography. "You need your teammates and the goodwill of your competitors, too." Lance's teammates were a pack of riders called the peloton. Their purpose was to lead the way, shielding Lance from the wind and stopping his competitors from moving ahead. Lance figures that by staying in front of him on a windy day, his teammates save him up to 50 percent of the work he'd have to do himself. This allows him to save his energy for the moment when it's time to break out of the pack and race on ahead.

A support car travels along the race route. It carries, among other things, extra bikes and water bottles. Lance's coach travels in a second car with a radio transmitter. He sends instructions to the cyclists, warning them of road hazards or bad weather ahead. He also tells them when to break away from the pack and take the lead.

By 1996, things were definitely looking up for Lance. He was twenty-five and under contract with a French cycling team for a salary of $2.5 million for two years. He owned a beautiful home in Austin, Texas, and a fast, top-of-the-line sports car. That same year he won the 1,225-mile, 12-day Tour DuPont race in France. He was the first American ever to win that competition. The only race he still had not won was the world-famous Tour de France.

But something was wrong. Lance didn't look well, and he felt tired and achy much of the time. He ignored the signs of illness because he was used to putting up with pain. But there was definitely something seriously wrong.

One of his testicles was enlarged and painful. A few days after his twenty-sixth birthday, he developed a terrible headache. The next morning he couldn't see clearly. A few days later he coughed up a great deal of blood. Finally, he checked in with a doctor.

Test results were initially devastating. Lance Armstrong had cancer.

Tests showed that he had an aggressive form of testicular cancer that was already spreading throughout his body. His cancer had established itself in his stomach, his lungs, even his brain. Doctors gave him a 50/50 chance of survival.

# Chapter 4

# Ready for
# the Tour de France

**D**uring the last months of 1996,
Lance's entire focus was on surviving.
His cancerous testicle was removed and
he underwent chemotherapy treatments
to destroy the remaining cancer. He
underwent frequent tests to see if the
treatments were working. While

chemicals could destroy some of the malignant cells, doctors had to operate to remove those on Lance's brain.

The medical treatments had terrible side effects. Lance threw up a lot, lost his hair, and at times didn't have the energy to speak. Through all of this, his attitude was, "I want to live. Do whatever you must to get rid of the cancer." He even "talked" to his cancer, telling it, "You picked the wrong guy. When you looked around for a body to try to live in, you made a big mistake when you chose mine."

Lance returned home between treatments. Friends would visit and go out on bike rides with him. But the chemotherapy, while killing the cancer cells, killed healthy cells as well. There were times when Lance didn't think he would ever compete in racing again.

A month after his treatments ended, Lance announced the formation of the Lance Armstrong Foundation (LAF) to raise money for cancer research and education.

In 1997, Lance was declared cancer-free. But until he was cancer-free for a year, he wasn't completely out of danger. He started training again, but without much enthusiasm. He played golf and spent time working with the LAF.

Lance's first attempts to return to racing ended in exhaustion and depression. His lungs were badly scarred, and there was no guarantee that the cancer wouldn't reappear. He was afraid. But his coach, Chris Carmichael, encouraged him to get back in the race. Lance agreed to prepare for one more race in the United States.

Lance and Chris, along with a friend of theirs, went to Boone, North Carolina, where Lance had trained before. It was early April. "The first day was nice," Chris remembers. "But then the weather turned ugly." There was cold rain and wet snow. Lance was peddling to the top of Beech Mountain—it was a hard climb and a journey of more than 100 miles. Nobody knows exactly what happened on that ride. All of a sudden, Lance was in racing form! "Go, Lance, go!" Chris yelled from his car. At the top of the mountain he offered to load Lance's bike onto the car and drive him back. But Lance said, "Give me my rain jacket. *I'm riding back.*"

By 1998, Lance was back in serious competition. He was a member of the U.S. Postal Service Team. He was healthy again and seventeen pounds

*Lance Armstrong, leader of the U.S. Postal Service team, shakes hands with Bernadette Chirac, wife of French President Jacques Chirac*

lighter. Fighting cancer had taught him the value of life. Now he was ready to win the most important cycling competition of all—the Tour de France.

Chapter 5

# "A Simple Pleasure"

The Tour de France is a world-class sporting event—the supreme test of strength and endurance. Thousands of cars, buses, motorcycles, and helicopters observe the riders. At least 15 million people in France line the highways to see the cyclists whiz by.

The course changes slightly each year and passes through villages and city streets, over hills and into valleys, to end on the streets of Paris. It is so physically demanding that it's like running twenty marathons in twenty days, according to an article by Michael Spector in *The New Yorker* magazine.

The race takes place over a three-week period and a difficult course of approximately 2,200 miles. Each day of the race is called a stage, and there are twenty stages. The winner is the one who covers the entire course faster than anyone else. Each day a yellow jersey is given to the rider with the fastest time to date. He wears that famous yellow jersey until someone else's time beats his. The final winner of the race may come in only seconds ahead of the rider behind him.

There are rules of behavior. If someone falls, the riders he is with wait for him to get up, climb back onto his bike, and catch up. Food and water are passed to the riders during the competition.

When he's racing, Lance eats a hearty breakfast, then two heaping plates of pasta and a power bar three hours before the race. He prepares very hard before each Tour de France. "He works as if he is possessed," Chris said. He trains for endurance and speed. "It's a little bit nutty, in fact, what he puts himself through so that he can win each year." Knowing the route the race will take, Lance scopes it out so that he knows each curve and any problems that could arise.

It seemed impossible that Lance could win the Tour de France in 1999,

*Lance Armstrong (left) crashes in the*
*2003 Tour de France after a knapsack held*
*by a spectator was snagged on his handlebars*

after having survived cancer, but he did.
He won again the next year and the
next. In 2003 he was back, in hopes of
winning a fifth time in a row. With less
than week to go in the 2003 Tour de
France, Lance had a fifteen-second lead

over his closest rival, Germany's Jan Ullrich. Riding hard up a French mountain, Lance started sprinting ahead to pass Ullrich and a small group of other riders. Suddenly, a knapsack held by a spectator was snagged on his handlebars and Lance fell off his bike onto the asphalt. Ullrich and the other riders slowed to wait, but when Lance got back onto his bike, his foot slipped off the pedal, making him fall onto his top bar. Furious and in great pain, he sprinted past Ullrich to win that day's stage. It gave him a lead of 1.07 minutes over Ullrich.

The week before, Lance had escaped injury in a mass crash in which a teammate suffered a fractured collarbone. In addition, he was not quite over a virus. He seemed tired, and the weather was very hot. One brutally steamy day in the French Alps, two competitors tried to pass him. One of them lost control and crashed. Lance, who was behind the fallen man, swerved to the left and rode down a grassy slope across a switchback. He had to get off his bike and leap, bike in hand, over a ditch to rejoin the race.

On the next to the last day of the race, Lance was better prepared than his rival, Ullrich. Ullrich had not ridden the wet course in advance but had seen it on videotape. Lance did more than that. He drove the course, with his team director checking every treacherous corner and slippery roundabout. In the race, Ullrich crashed on a slick corner, losing fourteen seconds. The Tour de France ended with Lance coming in sixty-one seconds faster than Ullrich.

When he crossed the finish line in

Paris, Lance was quoted as saying, "If there's one thing I say to those who use me as their example, it's that if you ever get a second chance in life, you've got to go all the way."

In 2004, Lance raced to victory yet again, becoming the only six-time winner in the history of the Tour de France. On a brilliant July afternoon, he pedaled to the finish line on the Champs-Elysées in Paris, along with the other members of the U.S. Postal Service Team.

Lance's sixth Tour de France win elevated him above four five-time champions: Eddy Merckx of Belgium, Miguel Undurain of Spain, and Jacques Anquetil and Bernard Hinault of France.

Many observers judged that the 2004 race was Armstrong's best Tour to date,

*Lance Armstrong celebrates*
*yet another Tour de France Victory* ▶

with five solo stage wins and a team trial victory.

"It's as if I was with my five friends and we were thirteen years old and we all had new bikes and we said, 'OK, we're going to race from here to there,' " Lance told a reporter after the 2004 race.

"It was like that for me. A simple pleasure."

# Glossary

**Arrogant** – proud; overconfident; egotistical.

**Autobiography** – the story of a person's life, written by that person. (A *biography* is the story of a person's life written by someone else.)

**Boastful** – self-important; arrogant; proud.

**Cancer** – a disease that causes a growth to spread and cause damage to the body.

**Chemotherapy** – the use of chemicals to destroy cancerous growths.

**Contract** – a legal agreement between two people or groups of people that explains what each person or group must do for the other.

**Cooper Institute** – a nonprofit association that conducts research and educational programs focusing on exercise, health, and nutrition; founded in 1970 by Dr. Kenneth H. Cooper.

**Depression** – a state of feeling sad or low in spirits. Chronic depression can lead to serious psychological problems.

**Endurance** – the ability to continue a prolonged stressful activity.

**French Alps** – the portion of the Alps that runs along the southeastern edge of France. (The Alps are the highest mountain belt in Europe. They extend, in south central Europe, from the Gulf of Genoa to the Danube River in Vienna.)

**Germany** – a country in central Europe. (The capital of Germany is Berlin.)

**Malignant** – in medical terms, marked by cancer.

**Moscow** – a city in west central Russia; the capital of Russia.

**Paris** – a city on the Seine River in northern France; the capital of France.

**Rival** – in sports, an opponent in an athletic competition.

**Roundabout** – an indirect route or detour.

**Side Effects** – unintended, and usually unpleasant, consequences of a medical procedure or medication.

**Squad** – a small group or team engaged in a common effort.

**Switchback** – a road or trail with many steep uphill and downhill slopes and sharp turns.

**Testicular** – relating to the male reproductive gland.

**Time Trial** – a competition in which individuals are timed over a set course or distance.

**Tour de France** – a world-famous, 2,286-mile annual cycling race with a finish line in Paris. The first Tour de France was held more than a century ago, in 1903.

**Treacherous** – dangerous; risky.

**Triathlon** – a long-distance race consisting of three phases (as swimming, bicycling, and running).

**Virus** – the cause of an infectious disease.

**Willfull** – stubborn; obstinate; determined.